POWER OF MAKING

The importance of being skilled

Edited by Daniel Charny
V&A Publishing and the Crafts Council

First published by V&A Publishing, 2011

V&A Publishing
Victoria and Albert Museum
South Kensington
London, SW7 2RL
www.vandabooks.com

ISBN: 978 185 177 653 5

10 9 8 7 6 5 4 3 2 1
2015 2014 2013 2012 2011

A catalogue record for this book is available from the British Library.

Designed by Oscar & Ewan
Copyedited by Mandy Greenfield
Glossary by Anna Faherty

Printed in Italy

V&A Publishing
Supporting the world's leading museum of art and design, the Victoria and Albert Museum, London

Contents

*Deep-skin satellites
were developed
for the proliferation of
connecting tissue.*

Embroidered
surgical implant
Peter Butcher
Ellis Developments Ltd
UK (Nottinghamshire)
2005

Computer-aided design
and manufacture,
lockstitch machine
embroidery,
hand-stitching

Nitinol alloy wire

Foreword

The *Power of Making* is the second Victoria and Albert Museum and Crafts Council triennial exhibition.

The relationship between our two organizations is a fruitful one, with both committed to increasing awareness of, and challenging preconceptions around, craft and craftsmanship. And this exhibition enables us to demonstrate the importance, relevance and dynamism of craft in the digital age.

The international scope of the *Power of Making* highlights how the impulse to make things with our hands is universal. The action of making, and the outcome of a crafted object, connects cultures, communities and generations. Handmade objects have a story. They have been touched, manipulated, hammered, thrown, blown, carved by another human hand. They connect us to our past and to our familial and cultural histories. They are the objects that we see in the public collections of the V&A and the Crafts Council – recording, as elegantly as verbal and written accounts, the histories of cultures and peoples.

As we progress further into the twenty-first century the proliferation of social crafting groups has perhaps brought us full circle, highlighting a time when communities would have congregated to make things in each other's company. People are now using different ways to communicate, but the desire to make together in a social context is growing ever stronger.

The range of objects in the *Power of Making* shows how craft and the ingenuity and skill of makers across the world imbue our everyday lives. The tacit knowledge of material and the dexterity and skill of makers have an impact across many industries – from film, fashion, interiors and design to medical innovation through bio-implant embroidery, artificial eyes and glass prosthetics.

The *Power of Making* is a celebration of the empowering nature of making and the human instinct to create.

Rosy Greenlees, Executive Director, Crafts Council
Mark Jones, Director, Victoria and Albert Museum

Thinking of Making
Daniel Charny

This book, published alongside the V&A's and Crafts Council's *Power of Making* exhibition in September 2011, aims to encourage debate on the nature and importance of making. Seven hands-on thinkers help to explore key issues surrounding current attitudes to making.

Almost all of us can make. It is one of the strongest of human impulses and one of the most significant means of human expression. To some, making is the fountain that releases creative ideas; to others, making is about participating in society as well as defining personal identity. To most of those who make, though, it is likely that they do not think of it as creative activity. It is their way of making a living – an absolute necessity. The power of making, from the height of luxurious freedom to the depth of deprivation, is that it is something people can do.

While for some people making is critical for survival, for others it is a way of learning. And maybe also a way of defying conventions, enjoying life or solving its problems. Making serves other needs, too.

It allows people to take care of loved ones, worship, mourn, celebrate or demonstrate. It is a way of exercising (free) will.

Making is the universal infrastructure of creative production – be it technical or artistic, scientific or cultural.

Though intentions and conditions vary, all makers participate in the unique human experience that comes from being completely engrossed in creative activity. Being 'in the zone' is felt by a four-year-old as much as by a seasoned master.

Yet despite all the value that exists in making, fewer and fewer people know how to make the things they use, need or want; or even how these things are made. This is one of the unfortunate legacies of the Industrial Revolution that has shaped the world we live in. The distance between the maker and the user is growing and, with it, knowledge, understanding and appreciation are diminishing. This is true in all walks of life, and increasingly in many professional disciplines.

Distance and lack of understanding are impacting also on governments and educational institutions, which are failing to see that making is very much part of the future – that the power of making lies far beyond providing technical support to those who manage. Nor is making the exclusive domain of the creative arts. Applied thinking lies at the core of creating new knowledge of all kinds, and the sensibilities of making should increasingly be made a part of our future. If it is not, it will lead to a great loss in value. Arts should not be separated from science, technology, engineering and mathematics.

At the same time we are in a fascinating era, in which change is being driven by massive computational powers and social movements. New networks for sharing knowledge are creating new types of makers and fuelling new communities of practice. Crafts are mixing with digital practices and finding new audiences. Models of fabrication, production and distribution are being revisited. There are also those who advocate making rather than buying, in order to take care of the planet's limited resources. And growing numbers of people are interested in where their food, clothing, furniture, building materials and cultural products are coming from, how they were made and by whom. This sounds more like a renaissance than a requiem.

Whatever one may believe, most people involved in making see it as a continuum that must be protected and encouraged. To do that, more people need to better understand what goes into making and see how much of it is personal.

In all cases of making – be it whittling a bow and drill to make a fire; shaping a piece of timber to be cut by a computerized milling machine; carving a wooden last or splitting leather to make a shoe; moulding a prosthetic eye to fit its socket; inventing a new way to manipulate metal tubes to describe a figurative form; knitting lace underwear or stitching sequins onto a religious flag; or even programming a 3D printer to replicate its own parts – there are always two aspects that come into play. How can it be made? And how good are you at it? The first is a question about technique, the second a matter of personal skill.

These two aspects of power are what the exhibition is about. It includes many curious objects, which were selected to demonstrate human achievement in three areas: first, in developing extraordinary methods for making; second, in acquiring spectacular personal skills; and, finally, in devising ingenious experiments.

This publication addresses the same themes, through a slightly different approach. It is a compilation of commissioned essays and an interview, separated by images with short fictional captions. They are all here to suggest thoughts and references to cultural, social, educational, technical and creative processes of current aspects of making.

In the first essay, anthropologist Danny Miller reflects on contemporary attitudes to making. He celebrates an understanding of craft that does not denigrate industrial manufacturing. In view of the exhibition, he also revisits the role of the V&A as an institution that was founded on the principle of democratized participation, an ambition that is still relevant for future craft, design and technology.

Cultural historian, educationalist and writer Sir Christopher Frayling takes on one of the key historical manifestos for creative education and production: the founding manifesto of the Bauhaus. He argues that it has long been misunderstood. For Walter Gropius and his colleagues the crafts were not something romantic and nostalgic, but rather a way to look ahead. The time is right, he says, for art and industry to visibly embrace what crafts have become.

Researcher, curator and author Martina Margetts, in her essay 'Action Not Words', considers the role of making in the creative process. She maps out the argument that the role of making is to create new ways of thinking, through engagement with materials, techniques and ideas. Ultimately she proposes that making is 'a revelation of the human impulse to explore and express forms of knowledge and a range of emotions', with the reward of experiencing 'an individual sense of freedom and control in the world'.

'Social Making', by curator and researcher Ele Carpenter, comments on the meeting of craft practice and digital practice. Reviewing some of the new forums where people share knowledge of experimentation and get involved in collaborative production, she examines the reasons for de-skilling and shows how social networks enable makers of diverse interests to re-skill. New patterns of learning encourage people to get a deeper understanding of how material things work, and of how to build and repair them.

The digital potential combined with physical making could not be better represented than by the Director of the Center for Bits and Atoms, Neil Gershenfeld. In a recently conducted interview he describes how the now-sweeping network of Fab Labs started and what future ambitions this self-seeding movement has on its agenda. Gershenfeld explains how social engineering is just as fundamental to these technological-innovation learning environments as technical know-how, and talks of the next industrial revolution that could be coming out of Manchester.

In the last essay, science-fiction author and techno-culture speculator Bruce Sterling reflects on the future maker and on the culture of the 'mashup'. He envisions a new situation, where technology and hands-on tinkering are one, and the dominant activity is 'hacking the post-industrial milieu'. This will be a universal condition, he writes: 'No nation, people, institution, party or discipline is exempted from this transition.'

The images included in the book are a snapshot from the *Power of Making* exhibition; each set relates to the preceding article. The captions beside them, written by novelist Patricia Rodriguez, suggest inventive (even fictional) readings of the objects. The aim here has been to reflect some of the symbolic or emotional impact that is imparted through making.

Finally you will find a glossary of techniques and processes, inspired by those that were applied to the making of the objects in the exhibition. This useful list is the start of a resource that will hopefully serve future makers and grow as others feed back into it. For as long as people can learn from each other, individuality and society will be able to thrive. This starts with instilling confidence and a sense of independence, and runs through to creative innovation and mastery of precious knowledge. Full knowledge cannot be transferred solely through the sharing of information; it must be kept alive and passed on through the experience of making.

This is just as much a commercial proposition as it is a personal, social and cultural one.

Once you outgrow the discipline
of the warp and the weft,
your thread
starts trailing stories.

'The Tree of Life'
cross-stitch
Captain A. Casdagli, CBE
UK (London)
2006

Counted-thread
needlework,
freehand stitching

Stranded cotton on linen

Watch me go,
inside the belly of the big fish,
out of the trunk of a big tree,
into earth's hull.

Untitled (Red Fish)
Paa Joe/Kane Kwei Studio
Ghana (Accra)
2010

Photo courtesy
Jack Bell Gallery

Wood carving, painting

Wood

'Barnsby Aurora'
dressage saddle
Barnsby Saddles
UK (Walsall)
2010

Saddlery, pattern-cutting,
stripping

Leather, foam, wood
and metal

*A material description
of the missing volume
between two mammals.*

Tyre shark sculpture
Ji Yong Ho
South Korea (Seoul)
2007

Clay modelling,
fibre-reinforced plastic
moulding, paintwork

Used tyres, synthetic
resins

*Two predators
swapped skins
but one was more deadly
than the other.*

The Power of Making
Daniel Miller

The words 'cutting-edge' have never seemed more appropriate: more than 100 objects that speak of the skill of crafting, but which also seem to celebrate the joy of the contemporary, the unprecedented capacities of today. This is an exhibition with a simple message: go out and learn to make something, just because you can. Feel for yourself that sense of achievement and exhilaration when you see before you the finished object of your own labour, and how that object has in turn made you more than you otherwise had been.

At the same time the *Power of Making* exhibition is an act of rejuvenation within the context of the V&A, which at its core suffers from a paradox. The original title of this institution was not the Victoria and Albert Museum, but the Museum of Manufactures. It was dedicated to being (and remaining) cutting-edge in the very same sense as the *Power of Making*. Its establishment created a niche that was not defined by craft – in the sense of a nostalgia for lost skills or work – but by industrial arts that embraced the new potential of industrial manufacture and looked forward to carving out a terrain that was neither quite art nor industry, but something in between. The museum was meant to educate its audience, but also to encourage a more democratized participation in design and technology.

To achieve this, the Museum of Manufactures was intended not just to exhibit, but also to inspire its visitors to push the boundaries of manufacture and to envisage new worlds that would continue to delight future decades. These objects spoke of an unprecedented combination of labour, industrial power, inspiration and will. The subsequent paradox is that things within the Museum become historical merely by virtue of remaining in time. Exactly the same objects that began life as directional signs to the future now sit on the same plinth representing memorabilia of the past. The world has sped past them and has replaced the aura of promise with that of patina. If we want to regain and embrace that original spirit and intention, it will be through temporary exhibitions such as the *Power of Making*, which has cast a net across the shoals of the present and exhibits objects still dripping with contemporaneity.

For this purpose there is no need to repudiate the past. One of the first objects we encounter in the exhibition is a dry-stone wall, a reminder that most of our ancestors were involved in ordinary labour, mainly (but not entirely) associated with agriculture. We still meet and greet a litany of trades in the form of common English surnames: 'It's a pleasure to see you, Mrs Cooper', 'a fine day, Mr Sadler', 'well done, Master Taylor', 'begging your pardon, Ms Mason'. Several of the objects on display speak of ancient craft such as damascened steel, which we continue to value in the finest kitchen knives.

There is, then, no suggestion that we should forget long centuries of skill and labour. Indeed, these artisanal traditions are not separated out as memories. They are juxtaposed with contemporary decorative arts and with a celebration of machines intended to demonstrate the dynamism of industry – a future of machines that can make other machines. Nor should one be fooled into thinking that a printer that can take the simple drawing of a child and turn it into a three-dimensional object is just a toy. You see in such a tool a radical new future for industrial society. I strongly suspect that one day I will want to possess a 3D printer, just as I presently cherish my smartphone. This single object, the 3D printer, represents perhaps the most profound challenge to what we today call 'crafts', because we will be able to make things with it that presently can only be created by hand. Yet this exhibition is in partnership with the Crafts Council. It is a sign that craft has flourished by embracing the ethos of the Museum of Manufactures, rather than by remaining aloof from industry.

There has always been a struggle for the heart of craft, and it remains one of considerable importance, since it is a fight over the ideology of time itself. Craft can easily become a vehicle of nostalgia, whose primary purpose is not just to remind us of what we have lost, but thereby to imply that we are diminished in our very humanity. Since the Industrial Revolution there has been a mourning for the loss of manual labour, and a belief that what we have gained in the wealth of industrial commodities has been at the expense of the human spirit. A 3D printer is the Devil's gift, taking us still further from a glimpse of heaven. Such ideas seem designed to make us feel shallow and inauthentic by comparison with our ancestors, and probably increase rather than decrease our feelings of alienation.

This view was established through a genre of writing that goes back to the nineteenth century. From William Morris to John Ruskin and the Romantics, we have mourned our separation from labour. Even those with the best intentions and political motivation penned celebrations of manual labour that now seem pompous and leaden. The presumption was that the contemporary represents the end of a history of original craft that was richer and better. But the idea that once upon a pre-industrial time most people engaged in fulfilling manual labour is utter nonsense. Such writings tend to highlight those artisans, such as the very few jewellers, who had the freedom to innovate and delight in their work, mainly because they served elites and rulers. But beneath these lay millions whose handiwork was limited to tasks such as dry-stone walling or the hoops for making barrels. As an anthropologist, I have lived for several years with non-industrial farmers and potters. Such people are engaged in making a given range of objects over a lifetime, simply to feed their family. The modern ideals of creativity and fulfilment are simply not relevant in most cases. Working life is often as mindless and boring as serving any conveyor belt. And then, when your back is breaking from planting and weeding, or from gathering clay and beating earth, unseasonal weather destroys the crop, or the wrong kiln temperature breaks the pots. I am not at all surprised that almost everyone I worked with wanted to give up farming and manual labour for work they saw as more rewarding, including factory work. This is not history – this is the majority of today's population in China and India.

So a celebration of craft that denigrates industrial manufacture is an act of hypocrisy. It is precisely because we now have industry, where machines take over so many boring and repetitive tasks, that those who have emerged from impoverishment can afford to celebrate craft as something we do for pleasure and leisure. Ideals of creativity and self-fulfilment grew with the Machine Age. The *Power of Making* is dominated by objects that speak of the sheer fun, imagination and brilliance of these new crafts, which entice us to take part because we want to. They are not the results of the manual labour required of us to put bread on the table. The spirit is closer to the fine British tradition of amateurism and the democratization of skill, so that we can all look for a niche or hobby. We can hone a skill to take pride in making things, and revel in work that has no clear boundaries from the world of play. Many of these objects are present because of the way in which they show how skill can be used to have fun through mimicry, mockery, swapping one material for another unexpected alternative. We walk past the lace fence, the glass grenade, hand-crafted replica foods, 'glass'-blowing using sugar, bikes made from Swarovski crystal. We see people who just felt 'up' for the challenge of trying to make by hand things that we have assumed could only be fashioned by machine – the handmade camera, a bicycle created by someone who has previously only made boats.

So I do not see the *Power of Making* as a nostalgia for lost arts or a Luddite critique of industrial production. It doesn't seem to differentiate between, on the one hand, objects that require years of devotion and skill and, on the other, machines which ensure that even the ham-fisted and ill adept of us can make quite extraordinary things. Digital design and plastics can also be celebrated here, for the capacities that they now give to us all. Because, truth be told, many of us would like to be involved in making things, but would have been quite useless at many of the tasks on display here. The only thing we might have made is complete failures. I recall endless humiliations when I couldn't plane a piece of wood, failed to throw a pot, plucked the flowers and left the weeds, and was relegated to playing the triangle at school because I couldn't even keep up with playing the recorder. It was many years before I found some activities that I was just about 'good enough' at to enjoy, such as birthday-cake decoration and writing. The exhibition shows us fantastic constructions at which we gawp in awe, but the reason I want a 3D printer is to make the things I would never have been able to produce otherwise, however strong my desire. Programming such a device with, for example, instructions to add some personal detail could replace shopping for the generic.

The theme here, as in the original Museum of Manufactures, is rather the way in which industry, design and labour complement each other. It's a two-way process. There are also objects on display here, such as embroidered surgical implants, for which manufacturers have turned to handcraft simply because machines cannot reproduce the intricacy and refined eye of a craft skill. But there is also a recognition that where once imagination and innovation were a luxury reserved for elites, today a garden shed can become the site for making replica medieval weapons from latex or wooden toys, turned on our own lathe, to give as Christmas presents to nieces and nephews.

The brilliance of the Museum of Manufactures, which I see reflected in the *Power of Making*, was that it steered a finely balanced course between two dangerous sirens: the music of industry, on the one hand, but also of art on the other. It learned their tunes, but replayed them on its own new instruments. On the one hand, the Museum respected and was sometimes in thrall to industry, but highlighted what were called the decorative arts – which incorporated the more imaginative skills of design and craft – and opened them up for us all. But it also faced the other way, in respecting art, but envisaging another, much more democratic potential than that found within the rarefied realms of art itself. When we refer to the power of making it, there are actually two meanings to the words 'make it'. One seems rather more modest – merely informing you that it was my labour, time and effort. The other, which seems to be increasingly common, is when 'I made it' is a claim to achievement. I made it as an important person in the world. The emphasis is less on the 'it' that was made and rather more on the 'I'.

When we first wander around this exhibition the most powerful pull is in the direction of the second meaning of 'making it'. There are works here that are so spectacular that we feel they have 'made it' as art. These objects are generally riveting, they amaze and enchant. Wow! – did you see what they did with someone's hair? A dress made from cassette tape? How did they *do* that with just paper or wire? By the end we are asking ourselves if there is no end to our capacity to imagine, and no limits to our ability to realize these concepts in material form. These creators clearly delight in their achievement in manufacturing the fantastic from the most unlikely and obdurate materials. Crocheting a bear, making sculpture from coat hangers –the exhibition seems to grant such objects the imprimatur of the V&A. They have 'made it', alongside the likes of Ron Arad and Alexander McQueen. In turn they allow the V&A to challenge the finest art galleries, in showing us the most extraordinary and inspiring of creations.

The problem with this first encounter, and its accompanying amazement and enchantment, is that we can feel awed, but also excluded; only very special people can create such astonishing artefacts – the artists. But when we look again we realize that many of the things we have seen are actually not so special. They include eco- and wicker coffins that are more expressive of what we hope will be our modesty in the face of the environment. Other objects remind us of the mundane worlds of making, the walking sticks and samplers. There are the charming and self-effacing things made by peoples from all around the world, where the delight is not in genius, but merely in the shaping of materials into artefacts that adorn or facilitate our life. Where an art exhibition may subsume craft to aesthetics, here it is the other way round – there is a domestication of art taking place, a bringing down to recognizable labour. The work may be beautiful, but it is used to create a medical intervention. Extraordinary skill lies behind the prosthetics that give back a working limb or an artificial eye or a prototype. There is fancy and aesthetics, but here in service to utility.

We might be tempted to describe these objects as magical, but one of the key points of the exhibition is that they are not. These are not tricks and illusions. In almost every case we may have difficulty imagining how to make it, but we can see clearly what it is made from. The dress is revealed as having been woven from cassette tape, the portraits are three-dimensional, but still paper. Given the imagination and skill, such things are possible without magic or illusion. Merely knowing what can now be envisaged brings us closer to that other aim of the Museum of Manufactures: to educate. Today an education in the basics of production is needed more than ever. We have become extraordinarily distant from the sources of our own material culture. I used to teach a university class on basic technology, taking examples from South Asia. It was soon evident that students today could be entirely ignorant of how the very clothes they are wearing are made from spinning and weaving, how a pot is thrown or metal is cast, but equally what plastics are made from, and the difference between growing rice and growing wheat. The more things we possess and consume, the more the origins of those things are taken for granted. Why is it not part of our most basic education, at primary school, to learn the fundamentals of how most things are made and from what? As this exhibition reveals, it is only when the juxtaposition or material is distinctly odd that we are shocked into an awareness of the underlying technology.

The core of this exhibition lies not in art, but in craft – objects that relate not to the quick invention of conceptual art, but to the slow perfection of skill; the constant endeavour that allowed someone to become better and better at what they could do with materials. While the term 'art' conjures up the tortured bohemian, the critic, huge sums of money and even bigger egos, 'craft' returns us to something that in practice is often deeper, commonly requiring both collaboration with other people and collaboration with machines. It encompasses both industrial labour and things that can be made at home, as a form of relaxation from a day spent at work: embroidered jewellery, quilting and knitting in the living room, messy stuff in the shed. Some exhibits are unique, but others speak of crafts of popular culture that would not normally have 'made it' to the V&A as emblematic of art, yet are quite prominent in many high streets, such as nail art or fake food displays. Some objects have been made by grafting popular culture onto craft, as with hybrid Wedgwood and Cola.

It's not all fun; reborn babies may be poignant, but are pretty creepy. Nor should it be possible to stand in a field of objects, many of which are consumer goods and commodities, without the pricking of conscience. The green objects remind us that there does need to be an end to quantity – at least of those objects that are not ultimately sustainable from an environmental perspective. Every now and then we find ourselves in places such as Rwanda and Haiti. Suddenly we are

A FINELY BALANCED COURSE BETWEEN TWO DANGEROUS SIRENS

thinking of a much wider world, including countries that are otherwise banished to mere 'Made in...' labels hidden in the clothes or ornaments we buy, which protect us from views of exploitation and from our own role and responsibility for a world in which the demand for cheaper and cheaper goods ends up somewhere as competition for lower- and lower-paid labour.

These concerns resonate with the core theme of craft because both are founded in the art of care. The care that we take in making something properly is cousin to the care that we retain for other people and their labour, and to a care and concern for our environment and its future. It is a common conversational trope to suggest that we live in a superficial and transient world. We don't at all. We live in a world that constantly tempts us to be superficial and transient because there is so much of it. So many things we could do and give attention to. But there is nothing to stop us making selections, narrowing our attention and selecting depth at the expense of breadth – opting for patience and seeking skill. By a certain age most people you meet have found some little plot or computer screen from which to cultivate some depth to themselves. So if you can be bothered to come with them to their allotment or their room (or perhaps now their YouTube or URL) and gain their confidence, they might shyly reveal and take pride in what they have created.

Much of my academic life has been an attempt to acknowledge that there can be skill and craft and production, even in the midst of consumption. The word 'bespoke' attached to several of these exhibits links the personal in production with the personal in consumption.

I would go further still and value the crafts of everyday life: being good at putting on make-up before going to work in the office, at spotting a promising football player so that you can impress your mates in the pub, at assembling just the right combination of clothes from your wardrobe or at planning an expedition that makes all the children equally happy. An attitude that only celebrates the crafts-people who have 'made it', but fails to recognize the way that all of us, every day, strive to do some things well, ignores the breadth as well as the depth of skill and craft in modern life.

So this exhibition is actually itself a fine act of craftsmanship, conceptually as well as physically. It neither excludes art at one end nor industry at the other. It follows the Museum of Manufactures in camping out on the middle ground, where you don't need to be an artist or to have a factory. All you need to do is to remind yourself that producing things is one of the most effective means for the realization of the person, for seeing one's own capacity in the evidence of the things we have ourselves created. We all make things all the time: we cook meals, we write essays, we decorate rooms, we craft play-lists on iPhones for dance parties, we may even sew or carve. Inspired by this exhibition, we think about what we could do with Lego or Swarovski, or through miniaturization or unexpected juxtaposition. Maybe not a bamboo car, but I am suddenly wondering if I could do more with pasta than just eat it?

Square frame camera
Hyun-Seok Sim, CamerAg
Korea (Seoul)
2007

Precision metal engineering: lathing, filing, drilling, tapping

Sterling silver, glass, spring steel, 20-carat gold

The mechanism for memory steals your view, with just a click.

Start with the most affable stone,
all the ones laid after
chosen
for the stones found before.

The soloist's hands
were furious and fickle
or perhaps just indecisive.

Handmade shotguns
Watson Bros, Gunmakers
UK (London)
2010

Striking up the barrels, carving wood, tinning, barrel filing, brazing, lock-making, engraving, checkering, finishing

Turkish walnut, steel

Shoulder is to wood
what wood is to metal,
what trigger is
to your index finger.

'Fairies and goblin land' fingernail art
Kirsty Meakin
UK (Stoke-on-Trent)
2010

Freehand painting and sculpting

Nail-art products, acrylic paint, acrylic liquid and powder UV gel

Female deities
weigh down their hands
with ice-age follies and festive motifs.

'Cabana' cabinet
Fernando and
Humberto Campana
Manufactured by
EDRA, Italy
Brazil (São Paolo)
2010

Wood work,
metal work

Aluminium,
fire-proofed raffia

*Put away the tired familiarity
of your possessions.
Make a discovery
every time you reach for them.*

'Widow dressmaker'
pin dress
Susie MacMurray
UK (Cheshire)
2009

Courtesy Manchester
City Galleries
Photo by Ben Blackell

Black nappa leather,
43 kg adamantine
dressmaker's pins,
tailor's dummy

*They say a little prick
from the seamstress
is a sign of good luck.*

'Anemone' hat
James Lock & Co. Ltd
UK (London)
2010

Millinery

Textile, straw, sinamay,
goose feathers

*To confound
even the most imperious mind-reader,
deploy a plume of coral,
a reef of white smoke.*

'We must all turn to the crafts'
Professor Sir Christopher Frayling

In the first manifesto of the Staatliches Bauhaus (1919), the so-called 'handicraft' manifesto, with its angular woodcut cover of a tall cathedral of the arts by Lyonel Feininger, Walter Gropius wrote one of the great catchphrases of modern art and design education: 'Artists, architects, sculptors,' he declaimed, 'we must all return to the crafts.' Or so say most British studies of the first phase of the Bauhaus. An end to art for art's sake! An end to the art that has no living link with the realities of materials and techniques! A beginning – the beginning – of the unity of all the creative arts within the new architecture, mother of the arts, based in the experimental workshop!

It is a catchphrase which has – since that time – often been set in opposition to Marcel Duchamp's equally famous line, 'It's art if I say it's art.' After all, some commentators have said, Gropius's first manifesto anchors art practice in 'a return to the crafts' – and is thus the great polemical antidote to all those readymades, conceptual extravaganzas, assemblages, visual gags and performances that have overflowed from Duchamp's urinal. The polar opposite of Damien Hirst's recent confession that whenever he hears the word 'skill' he immediately thinks of macramé.

Or is it?

Actually, the phrase 'we must all return to the crafts' – which has fitted like a nice, woolly tea-cosy over much Anglo-Saxon thinking about the subject – is a mistranslation. What Gropius really wrote was 'we must all turn to the crafts': meaning the contemporary crafts, not some romantic, nostalgic vision of what they were once like, and how hard they were. Not a return, or even a U-turn, but a straightforward 'turn'. Like a philosophical turn in an argument, expressed in physical and visual terms. It was, as Gropius later added during the second phase of the Bauhaus, a question of the crafts shedding their 'traditional nature' – which was holding them back – and becoming instead 'research work for industrial production, speculative experiments in laboratory-workshops where the preparatory work of evolving and perfecting new type-forms will be done'. This was the turn that so impressed Herbert Read in his influential book *Art and Industry*, which helped to extend the argument in Britain from the craft workshop to productive industry, from hands-on making to research. In Germany, the shedding of the crafts' traditional nature had become politically urgent too, because popular anti-modernism was beginning to be channelled by the Far Right – unlike in Britain, where it was more associated with the rise of Socialism.

And yet almost every British book about the Bauhaus still prefers to interpret the manifesto as a plea for the skills of yesterday, to help artists find their way through the mega-visual confusions of today. Didn't Gropius also write that he was 'determined to transfer into practice' the ideas of his mentors John Ruskin and William Morris? And wasn't Walter Crane's 1890s curriculum for the Royal College of Art the origin of the Bauhaus progression from 'basic course' to 'specialized craft' taught by an artist and a technician? The Arts and Crafts Movement cast a very long shadow – and, by the way, it still does.

Walter Gropius resigned in 1928 in part because of the unsolved problem of 'turn' and 'return', craft and industry, artists and craftspeople, making and methods. His well-designed manifesto had made the issue seem so clear-cut, when in day-to-day reality it was much more messy. And in art education we have been arguing about it ever since, accelerated by the arrival of digital technology since the 1980s. Today, at a time when laboratory work in school science is becoming an endangered species, when 'design' has been transformed into a briefing (as crafts, design and technology have morphed into design and technology) and when craft workshops have been deemed too expensive, dirty and probably in breach of health-and-safety regulations, the debate has taken on a fresh urgency. There is talk of reviving long-forgotten technical schools (reviving again!). There is public debate within tertiary education about whether the crafts belong in the vocational sector or in universities. A coalition-government minister has recently argued that too many crafts 'have been given an academic veneer ... [which] has done academic study no favours'. The implication is that it would be better to put them back into the vocational box where they belong. The crafts, it is said, have developed since the 1960s a Cinderella complex, when they should be content to stay in the kitchen: far too many invitations to the ball have already been sent out. On the other hand, some educationalists have argued about schoolwork that the 3Rs should really be 'reading, wroughting, rithmetic' – rather than 'reading, writing, rithmetic', really the two skills of literacy and numeracy – and that 'making' and 'performing' must lie at the heart of any well-rounded education. Teaching creativity is one thing, but what about teaching anything creatively?

In order for this debate to progress beyond 'the shock of the new', the muddles that go right back to the Bauhaus – and beyond the Bauhaus to the Arts and Crafts Movement – really do need to be sorted out. The crafts must finally shed their nostalgic connotations (or, as Gropius put it, their 'traditional nature') in the teeth of countless advertising campaigns and television clichés to the contrary; they must even shed their ethical connotations (hard work is good for you) and be more comfortable with fluency in a contemporary language. They must come to terms with modernity – with the possibilities of digital technologies (for example, 'industries of one'), with urban living, interior design, the lifestyle pages, product design, architecture's close-up zones, the shifting borders of art at one end of the spectrum and design at the other, with all the colours and materials of the rainbow and with the outer limits of function.

A lot of craftspeople have crossed this river of fire to appropriate William Morris's phrase a long time ago. But public perception, and a lot of policy-makers, have yet to catch up. In addition to shedding their associations with 'the world we have lost', makers and teachers of the crafts must get used to articulating what is special about them – from an educational point of view – much more clearly.

My introduction to craft as a form of knowledge, which differs from the usual modes of classroom teaching, came from reading Book III of Jean-Jacques Rousseau's educational treatise *Émile* (1762) at an early age. *Émile* is a strong polemic, cast in the form of a story about a boy and his tutor, against learning by rote and social conditioning and in favour of the development of the individual child – what would today more prosaically be called, after Jean Piaget, 'the psychogenetic educational principle'. Book III of *Émile*, dealing with the early teenage years (which is when I first read it), is concerned with the learning of a craft, in Émile's case carpentry: 'If, instead of making a child stick to his books, I employ him in a workshop, his hands work to the advantage of his intellect, he becomes a philosopher while he thinks he is simply becoming an artisan.'

This linking of the hand and the head made a deep impression on me – at a time when everyone else seemed to be treating them as separate spheres – and I have often revisited *Émile* since then. But it raises the question 'in what sense a philosopher?' What is distinctive about craft knowledge as a contributor to the intelligence of feeling? Why is 'making' so important, at a time when in wider society deep learning of any kind – deep learning that takes time and patience – does not command nearly as much respect as it used to; and when technologies seem to be driving a wedge between makers and things? The potter and author Edmund de Waal has recently written of 'that epiphany when you see what you have made and it is different from

PUBLIC PERCEPTION, AND A LOT OF POLICY-MAKERS, HAVE YET TO CATCH UP what you had conceived'. Where exactly is that epiphany? It's a good question.

In my view, what continues to distinguish the crafts, to make them highly visible, is the care with which they have been made, the fact that they have been made by one human being for another, the individual 'take', the use of materials and the thoughtfulness of their design: design with attitude. And, yes, the patient mastery of technique until it becomes second nature. The crafts have become a wide range of possibilities, a spectrum, and the more inclusive and varied and versatile, the better. They can represent an ethical statement, but the point is that they needn't.

They need to turn, not return.

'Spun' chair
Heatherwick Studio
UK (London)
2010

Rotational plastic moulding

Aluminium

*For limbs
and mind to rest,
restlessness is required.*

Ministerial box
Barrow & Gale
UK (London)
2009

Getty Images

Hard shell covered in
roan leather, brass lock

Encase
the shifty matter
of shifting matters of state
from one tribulation to the next.

'Alphabet'
pencil-tip sculptures
Dalton Ghetti
USA (Connecticut)
2003-6

Photo by Sloan T.
Howard Photography

Carving

Wood, graphite

When you are down to the last inch
and think you are running out of possibilities,
sharpen your eye.

L-shaped suitcase
Sarah Williams
Williams British Handmade
UK (Herefordshire)
2009

Plywood, green bridle
leather, brass

*The discerning traveller
challenges
cabin baggage restrictions
on an irregular basis.*

'Bio-Suit'
extra-vehicular activity
space suit
Professor Dava Newman
(inventor), Trotti and
Associates, Inc. (design),
Dainese (manufacture)
Man Vehicle Laboratory,
Massachusetts Institute of
Technology
USA (Massachusetts)
2008

Photo by
Douglas Sonders

Polymers,
spandex and
nylon

*Hoping to encounter
hostile environments –
gaseous, telluric, cosmic
singularities.*

Knitted 'Aran rug'
Christien Meindertsma
Netherlands (Rotterdam)
2010

Photo by Reineke Otten

Knitting

Merino wool

*The sleepless knitter
counted enough sheep
to engulf the entire room
in one night.*

Handmade lace G-string
Koniakow co-operative
Poland (Koniakow)
2009

Lace-making: circle
pattern technique

Cotton thread

*When compulsion
had adorned every domestic surface,
it crocheted onto
the undomesticated.*

Action Not Words
Martina Margetts

What is the role of making in the creative process? This essay proposes that making is a revelation of the human impulse to explore and express forms of knowledge and a range of emotions; an impulse towards knowing and feeling, which shapes human action and hence the world we create. The reward of making is the opportunity to experience an individual sense of freedom and control in the world. Making is therefore not only a fulfilment of needs, but of desires – a process whereby mind, body and imagination are integrated in the practice of thought through action.

This mind/body interrelation, a phenomenological perspective grounded in the philosophy of Husserl, Heidegger and Merleau-Ponty, restores the mind/body split of Descartes, whose privileging of maths and science as the only verifiable processes denied bodily knowledge its significance in the world.[1] Already in Greek myth Paracelsus believed that in order to produce effects, 'humans must bring their bodies into the work'.[2] This idea of 'effects' achieved by making is central to the impact of everyday things, as this exhibition shows. Making is based on a sequence of repetitious acts, incrementally forming objects with meaning – 'imitation as a learned bodily habit that became a cognitive practice and finally led to knowledge and the production of effects'.[3]

This is the hidden embodied knowledge of making, dangerously disregarded by government policy-makers.[4] It expresses the kind of intelligence that the developmental psychologist Howard Gardner felt should be acknowledged when he critiqued the 'sharp distinction between the "reflective" and the "active"', a 'divorce between the "mental" and "physical"' so detrimental to societal progress and well-being: 'Only if we expand and reformulate our view of what counts as human intellect will we be able to devise more appropriate ways of assessing it and more effective ways of educating it.'[5] The *Discours admirables* by the sixteenth-century potter Bernard Palissy reveals the significance of Gardner's view. Palissy writes a dialogue between Theory and Practice on the production of glazed ceramics, wherein the latter says: 'Even if I have a thousand reams of paper to write down all the accidents that have happened to me in learning this art, you must be assured that, however good a brain you may have, you will still make a thousand mistakes, which cannot be learned from writings.'[6]

Theory, though regarded as superior, did not have the powers of observation, the material skills or the stamina to find the exact doses of the enamel ingredients that Palissy insisted on, through the voice of Practice: 'you should work to find that dose, just as I have done; otherwise you would esteem the knowledge too lightly'.[7]

Palissy's tale shows that excruciating years of labour eventually produced results and, with them, an autonomous, emotional and economic control over well-being. Tacit knowledge is still 'esteemed too lightly' in the contemporary world, though a recent flurry of texts and exhibitions such as this one are altering public perceptions;[8] and there is, too, the recognition of making as in itself producing happiness, 'flow' and pleasure, experienced by the maker and transmitted through the work to the viewer.[9] This is a crucial role of the 'power of making', offering an interaction with the spectacle of everyday things, which changes us and enhances life.

Everyday useful things play a major part in this exhibition, which through their virtuoso making produce extraordinary effects – hair, clothes, bikes, weapons, boats, food – evidence of the makers' extreme engagement with almost fetishized repetitive acts and spectacular material manipulations. Embodied in making is the operation of time and memory, with which the mind's eye, hand and tool draw on a profound well of tacit knowledge to originate form, sometimes in slow and patient incremental steps, sometimes in an instant. A contemporary Japanese swordsmith remarks, 'It's the split-second intuitive decision to remove the iron from the fire, when and how to bring up the flame, to immerse the blade in the water now – it is these acts of intuition that produce a sword.'[10] This is the 'workmanship of risk',[11] which David Pye, woodworker and theorist, characterizes as the foundation of individual craftsmanship, a crucial realization and transmission of the self within the object, a repeated affirmation of the conscious coming-into-being of the person and the thing.

Tools and equipment are prosthetic extensions of the body that carry the thought of the maker, wholly different from the autonomous production of machines. As Virginia Postrel recounts in *The Substance of Style*, 'Modernity itself is constructed not by sight alone but by the processes which the individual achieves through action.'[12] The construction of cities, colonization, domestic labour and cultural excellence rely on the ability to make things. 'Design is everywhere and everywhere is designed.'[13] The hand's sensitivity, developed over time, allows it to take the mind beyond its plan.

The plan of a design alters in the doing or, conversely, the beginning of making with the hands enables a plan to evolve. An unexpected deformation can appeal as much as the perfect fetish finish (compare, for example, the Lobb shoes with those of Marloes ten Bhömer, or recall the Spring/Summer 2010 shoes by Alexander McQueen).

WORK-
MANSHIP
OF RISK

Imagination is an ineffable part of process, so that both a collectively made Ghanaian coffin and chairs by Ron Arad can transcend the utilitarian requirements to embrace both subjective and objective elements of making. Such works, alongside medical exhibits and the productions of 3D digital printers, show that contemporary making relies on an accommodation between the handmade and the digital; in the exhibition a comparison can be made between a garment using Fabrican, the Woolfiller clothes and the woven-tape dress, showing how the specificities of choices in the making process set up different kinds of meaning.

Each choice reflects human identities and intentions. As Mark Smith discusses in *Sensory History*, the making process is enculturated: 'Sensory perception is a cultural, as well as a physical, act.'[14] There is no vacuum in production: making is achieved by a finely calibrated evolution of senses, in relation to each other and to different societies at different periods of history. The senses are not a 'natural' endowment or a hierarchy, but are learned, developed and entwined. This is echoed in Michel Serres's evocation of the senses as 'the ceaseless unravelling and reknitting of the body',[15] a different perception of knowledge formation from the more usual dominance of the linguistic. So the ideas of the mind are formed in the knowledge of the body, but just as the body contains and hides the mind and the emotions, so does the object shield its inner core. In the exhibition the surface of things excites with their speculative potentiality, a tantalizing state since we also want to know what lies beneath: here is the importance of making as an exploration of truth and illusion, the imperfect and the ideal.

Bernard Leach's contrasting words about making by non-Western and Western potters, as fundamental to cultural formation, can equally apply to the Ghanaian coffin and the Arad chairs:

> in the former case his period and its culture and his national characteristics will play a more important role than his personality; in the latter the chances are that personality will predominate. In either case sincerity is what matters, and according to the degree in which the vital force of the potter and that of his culture behind him flow through the processes of making, the resulting pot will have life in it or not.[16]

The role of making is therefore to give life to things, but also to show evidence of life within us, perhaps also at a spiritual level.

The role of making is a sequence of actions that set in motion a curiosity to go beyond what is already known, in a non-verbal language that extends our abilities to communicate with each other across cultures, time and space. It has been fashionable to indulge Roland Barthes's assertion of the 'death of the author' and Jacques Derrida's 'disappearing of the human being' in order for the participant to take control, but this exhibition shows a reversion. The maker has the freedom and control: the role of making is to create new ways of thinking, through engagement with the materials, techniques and ideas.

Michel Foucault asks, 'What is philosophy today ... it is not the critical work that thought brings to bear on itself? In what does it consist, if not in the endeavour to know how and to what extent it might be possible to think differently, instead of legitimating what is already known?'[17] Paul Valéry said that the hand is a philosopher.[18] So this exhibition shows that making is the only way that Foucault's exhortation to 'think differently' can ever be tangibly experienced in everyday life.

'Gorilla' coat-hanger
sculpture
David Mach, RA
UK (London)
2011

Steel coat hangers

Dry-cleaned and pressed?
Skeletal throwaways
amassed
a mighty mount of muscle mass.

'Rapidprototypedshoe'
Marloes ten Bhömer
UK (London)
2010

Photo by Marloes ten Bhömer

3D modelling, additive manufacturing

TangoBlack and VeroBlack polyjet resin

Start with basic shape and direction:
arrow-points-forward.
Be Mercury,
set wings to your heels.

'Fish out of water' bag
Lisa Farmer
Italy (Milan)
2011

Girogio Vacca (maker)
Lisa Farmer (designer)
Photo by Michelle Rossi

Leather working: cutting, folding, sewing, punching

Hand-sewn vegetable tanned leather

She used
the hollow body of the fish
to carry her remaining hours
of waterside patience.

'Cornflower centaurea
cyanus' ring
Nora Fok
UK (Hove, West Sussex)
2007
V&A: M.10–2008

Weaving, knotting, welding

Dyed and knitted nylon
monofilament

Borrow beauty from nature.
Appropriate
flora's fine filaments,
the electric hues of abyssal fauna.

'Gomli'
Ron Arad
UK (London)

© Ron Arad Associates
Courtesy Timothy Taylor
Gallery, London

Polyester gel-coat
and fibreglass

You might adopt
the shape of a teardrop
to go unnoticed in the wild.

For the corsair's tired eye
fine bone,
sailed back
from the shores of China.

proAesthetics Delft
eye patch
Damian O'Sullivan
Netherlands (Rotterdam)
2003

Photo by
Adriaan van der Ploeg

Modelling, glazing

Porcelain

Social Making
Ele Carpenter

Within contemporary creative culture there is a critical mass of makers organizing in response to the multiple crises of de-skilling, proprietary licensing and outsourced production. This eclectic mix of unlikely bedfellows is rapidly reshaping older patterns of 'Do It Yourself' production through both old and new technologies and 'Do It Together' networks,[19] both online and in located spaces. The makers are committed to open transparency and access to ideas and information. They use any tools or materials necessary. This approach acknowledges digital making as a craft, as discussed by Richard Sennett in *The Craftsman*.[20] Sennett argues that the open-source operating system Linux, for example, is a public craft because it is a tool that actively shapes the world around us through collective making.

Open-source digital-analogue hybridity is all about craft articulated through the language of technology: reverse-engineering to find out how things work, making your own tools, making the process public, learning through peer-to-peer skill-sharing. In media-art this distributed creativity is exemplified by Furtherfield's Visitors' Studio,[21] where people can work collaboratively online. Collective making is also embodied in the world of craft: the social skill-share event of the sewing circle, round-robin quilts made through international networks of patchworkers, and community-embroidered local histories. Garden-shed inventors take apart electrical goods and build new devices. Hackers build their own tools and modify software to their own needs. But these practices are no longer marginalized hobbyist crafts. They have entered the realm of amateur production with their own networks, expertise and knowledge-sharing, along with new forms of status building and cultural capital.[22] The intelligence of making is both material and conceptual: from the mathematics of patchwork or textual encoding of embroidery to the use of online networks to organize located events such as the Circle Line knitters[23] or Stitch 'n' Bitch meet-ups. Go along to any Maker Faire and you'll meet the practitioners, learn some skills, get online with folk. Dress up with steampunks and you've got the DIY props for a glamorous life of sci-fi handmade technology complete with goggles.

Today the 1990s Media Tacticalists and 2000s Craftivists might be mildly bemused, watching their ideas evolve into the mainstream, witnessing their labour being commodified without acknowledgement. A generation of crafters is obsessed with knitted cakes, and user-generated content is the media. Even Fendi have cashed in on the maker culture with their DIY needlepoint handbag.

But within this muddle of hobby-pop craft, the DIY enthusiast is re-skilling, breaking gender-codes in the process. She may be an artist, programmer, crafter, steampunk, geek; she may be a scientist, knitter, engineer, hacker, dork. Her conceptual frameworks respond to the politics of contemporary visual culture, where making can be a heady mix of amateur practices, reverse-engineering tools and utopian gestures. Reverse-engineering involves going carefully backwards through a production process. The problem of de-skilling means that this may sometimes be the only way to find out how something is made.

Knitters are networked through ravelry.com, while electrical experimenters meet up at Dorkbot,[24] an international community composed of 'people doing strange things with electricity'. Dorkbot brings together inventors, artists, scientists and engineers to showcase their work and swap stories. What is extraordinary about this community is that it sees electronics and software as materials to be reworked, rather than simply as end-user products. In London, MzTEK[25] examines how women are often marginalized in techie maker culture (somewhere in the technical communication it is often assumed that women are not really interested). This group of women artists and techies facilitates making and coding events, for women to learn the tools and concepts of the digital crafter-maker. It also runs workshops showing how to use tools such as the Arduino microprocessor, as demonstrated in the 'Tilt Sensing Quilt' by Plusea.[26] The Arduino is an open-source electronics platform that enables people to programme and create their own interactive objects and artworks.

Instructions for making the 'Tilt Sensing Quilt', and many other objects using the Arduino, are publicly available on the Instructables website. Here the 'How To' document is expanded into easy steps. This massive commitment to sharing and contributing knowledge to the public domain is a key characteristic of today's digital-craft maker culture. Underpinning the movement is the notion of the commons: common ownership and common access. The idea comes down to us from the English Diggers who, in 1649, took direct action to farm common land to protest against the privatization of land. In the 1960s the San Francisco Diggers practised free culture, including free shops, printing and publishing. And today alternative production and distribution models are explored through the Creative Commons, where digital material can be licensed to share rather than to own. The Creative Commons licences use clauses such as 'share-alike', and grant permission for others to remix content and make new 'derivative' works.

The digital world both enables and requires new models of production and distribution, such as ordering 'print-on-demand' objects, or making design blueprints 'open-source' to establish market share, encourage standardization or improve portability. Open Design is a catch-all term for a myriad of processes that enable transparency and/or collaboration at different stages of production. By enabling knowledge-sharing and knowledge-building, designs can easily be modified for localized use, typified by the MakerBot 3D printer, 'an open hackable robot for making nearly everything'.

Makers are not Luddites. They recognize that de-skilling is not simply the result of digitization, but an effect of the geo-political exploitation of technologies for profit over social or environmental sustainability. In response, re-skilling needs to take place across both digital and craft practices. In the same way that the cooper's barrel-making skills need to be shared for continuity, so the ability to programme code as a material needs to be taught in schools. Otherwise the result is end-user passivity, associated with product-loyal consumers who lack the skills for making, communication or survival. Embracing digital making as a craft enables space for experimentation and collaborative production as well as an in-depth understanding of how things work, and how to build and repair them. The maker culture is finding innovative ways to use, reuse and recycle the technologies and materials that we already have, from wood and textiles to electronics and digital devices.

'MakerBot Thing-O-Matic' 3D printer
Bre Pettis, Adam Mayer
and Zach 'Hoeken' Smith
USA (New York City)
2010

Photo by David Neff

Painted birch, custom
hardware and electronics

*Let your Bot
show You
exactly
what You mean.*

'Fendi Needlepoint Stitch
Baguette' embroidery kit
Italy (Rome)
2009

Sheer woven raffia, taupe
leather, embroidery
thread, needles, thimbles

*This status symbol is subject to
your personal dexterity.
This does not affect
your misconception of exclusivity.*

Tilt-Sensitive Quilt
Hannah Perner-Wilson
USA (Massachusetts
Institute of Technology)
2010

Fusing, machine and
hand-embroidering,
felting, etching and
painting

Assorted conductive
and non-conductive
fabrics and threads,
LilyPad Arduino, 8-channel
multiplexers, Bluesmirf
Bluetooth, 3-7v LIPO
battery

*My blanket knows it
when I can't sleep.
Every move, stretch, twitch, blink,
my blanket feels.*

Chainsaw-powered
sago grinder
Mombrasar Family
Blacksmiths
Indonesia (Tempat Garam,
West Papua province)
2008

Welding, engineering

Steel

A roaring shortcut
from trees to food.
Circular motion
from logging to nutrition.

Brewery barrel
Alastair Simms
UK (Wiltshire)
2010

Steaming, trussing,
dressing out, head-cutting

Wood, metal

He knew of a kind of precision
beyond measures.
The temperament of tools and materials –
his watertight secret.

'Picnic bench,
bats and ball'
Gareth Neal
UK (London)
2010

Photo by Sophie
Mutevelian

3D computer drawing,
computer numerical
control, marquetry
and veneering

Hard woods

*In a tiebreak situation
players might resort
to creating diversion with
their intricate duelling racquets.*

The Making Revolution
Professor Neil Gershenfeld in
conversation with Daniel Charny,
24 March 2011

A Fab Lab (fabrication laboratory)[27] is a fully kitted fabrication workshop which gives everyone in the community, from small children through to entrepreneurs and businesses, the capability to turn their ideas and concepts into reality.

The first Fab Lab was set up by MIT's Center for Bits and Atoms (CBA), which is directed by Professor Neil Gershenfeld and:

broadly explores how the content of information relates to its physical representation. The Fab Lab program has strong connections with the technical outreach activities of a number of partner organizations, around the emerging possibility for ordinary people to not just learn about science and engineering but actually design machines and make measurements that are relevant to improving the quality of their lives.[28]

Daniel Charny **I just had a look on your site at the number of Fab Labs around the world and it's amazing.**

Professor Neil Gershenfeld Well, it's hard for us to count, and it's unplanned, but I think it's approaching 100 now. From inner-city Boston to bottom-row India. The original goal was just one lab. Since then the number has doubled every year.

Can we start with a bit about the history of your approach, and talk through the philosophy that led to the start of this phenomenon?

Historically, hardware and software used to be segregated by discipline. So physical science was separated from computer science. But one of the themes that emerged from joint research is the idea of digitizing fabrication. That sounds easy to understand, but it's widely misunderstood. In the 1950s MIT [Massachusetts Institute of Technology] connected the first early computers to a machine tool to develop numerically controlled machining. So the concept of a computer connected to a tool is decades old. The key step-change was when Claude Shannon took us from analogue to digital communications and then, with a bigger group, Von Neumann and others from analogue to digital computing. This meant that by computing and communicating with discrete symbols you could correct errors. It took us from telephones to the Internet, from rotating gears to the computer in front of you.

In the 1950s the tools and the materials were analogue. With today's frontier of 3D printing, it's still analogue: you still 'smoosh' material around. In biology the heart of how proteins are built is digital. They have discrete elements that are built with codes. There's a good analogy with Lego: Lego is more accurate than the child, it corrects errors. And it's reversible. You can dissemble as well as assemble it. And those properties are also how biology works.

Lego, beyond the activities and behaviours it suggests, is still a kit of parts,

which needs to be put together. To continue the analogy, are you talking about self-building Lego or, in a way, self-producing Lego?

The core theme of our research on digital fabrication is not about computers controlling tools, but about the computer itself as a tool. And it's not just about programs describing things, but about things actually becoming programs – about putting codes into material. Look ahead 20 years and it leads to the *Star Trek* 'replicator' idea, the assembler that makes anything, from the atoms up. What's widely missed is that it's essentially an exercise in embodying codes and computers and materials.

What was the incentive to take the research outside your labs? How did you decide where they would be?

Fab Lab's initial trigger was a simple one. The core facility was funded by the National Science Foundation. They had a social-impact policy, and so they told us we had to show social impact. But we didn't just want to make a website or a class. We thought it would be more fun to provide tools. The idea was that we would spend tens of millions of dollars on campus, and in 20 years the tools would fit in your pocket. The Fab Lab on the other hand was about $50,000 in equipment, maybe $10,000 or $20,000 in materials. And that was all.

We opened the one lab in Boston, and then there was a strong link to a community in Ghana, which led to a lab going there. Then there was a strong link to South Africa... And every time we open a lab there are suddenly 10 more. But it's not our plan. People need these in their communities – for a range of reasons. Nobody's pushing and there isn't a formal process. People pull, and that's how it spreads.

Were you thinking at the time about how it might grow?

Well, there is a technical road map. Stage one is computers controlling tools. Stage two is machines that make machines. Stage three is building with materials containing codes. And stage four is building with materials containing programs. But we didn't have a support road map at the start. It was just about setting up one lab.

In retrospect it's like tracing the line from computer mainframes to PCs. Mainframes were followed by mini-computers, like DEC PDPs [programmed data processors] the size of a room, costing tens of thousands of dollars. That's when email and Internet, and most of the things you do on a computer, happened. Then along came devices like the Altair 8800. In a sense, Fab Labs are roughly the cost and complexity of DEC PDPs. So, historically speaking, we're analogous to when the Internet was invented.

Any one lab doesn't have the critical mass to tackle the questions we're asking. As the labs progress, what's emerging is .org and .com and .edu components. We initially created one, but that didn't work. It had to be distributed, a network of Fab Lab foundations. The idea is to provide aid all over the world – in inner cities and in conflict zones, in overdeveloped as well as underdeveloped regions. Because no one else is really providing tools for invention.

When did this social agenda kick in so strongly?

Right from the beginning, but there's a second piece: education. We have amazing kids – kids outstripping local educational opportunities with the tools in the lab. And we have a broadband video network connecting them. Rather than training them, exciting them and then telling them they have to go far away, we're teaching distributed classes through the lab network.

Is this centralized or nodal? What part of this is coming from the labs?

It has three components. There's a shared online component, broadband video, so everybody sees everybody and works in groups with peers and instructors. That's Fab Academy.

And there are businesses emerging where they don't just make and sell locally. The designs can be made anywhere in the world. They can be made locally, or they can be designed locally and then made anywhere. So you're shipping data, instead of shipping products.

And above all this are the research projects, which aren't in any one site, but are distributed around the network. So it really functions not as a centralized organization, but as a fundamentally distributed organization.

It seems to me that Fab Labs do something designers have long talked about, an agenda of fewer partitions. With direct contact between makers, designers, as well as with users, and with an idea of production as distribution. Are these some of your goals?

It is really important to be clear that this whole agenda isn't mine. It isn't written and it isn't planned. As regards designers, I did a keynote speech a few years ago in the US, at the annual meeting of the design community. It was an interesting experience.

I yelled at the audience, because – in a world of digital and personal fabrication – design as a discipline doesn't make sense. You can segregate hardware, software, logic, form, function, surface and code. But design spans all those levels of descriptions. The follow-up session was jammed out the door. Some people were in tears – not grumping, but saying, 'All my life that's what I wanted to do, but they wouldn't let me.'

It sounds like you've done shortcuts that other people are excited about, but don't entirely understand.

All my life I've been doing things like this. I tried to go to vocational school because I wanted to weld and fix cars, and I was told I couldn't, because I was smart. At Bell Labs I had union grievances because I tried to use workshop machines and was told, 'No, you're smart, so you have to tell someone else what to do.' I just never understood this.

So do you think there's potential in the Fab Labs to change learning environments in schools, or will they remain an independent network?

That's a tough question. To date we've avoided schools like the plague, due to all their constraints. But there are a number of Fab Labs emerging in school settings, thanks to some adventurous stakeholders who get what this is about and manage to do it without strangling it. I don't know the extent to which we are going to be able to change existing schools versus invent new schools. At a higher level at the Fab Academy, we are finding that we have to invent a completely new educational organization to keep this up.

Well, you called it an academy as opposed to a club or an institute...

That's because it's structured. We're giving degrees, diplomas and certificates. But we had to make them up. The analogy is to the integrity of the Cisco Networking degree and it is trusted because Cisco does networking and that's what people want. So the accreditors encouraged us to invent a degree, give it, make it have meaning and they would catch up with what we are delivering.

And what sort of people are generally involved?

There are young people, old people, technical, non-technical people, artists... It doesn't easily map onto any thumbnail description. What is clear is that some people know they want to do this, but many don't – they encounter it and then fall in love with it.

In that sense, do you think that – because it's to do with perception – a shift in attitudes is taking place?

Well, if you go to a community lab and ask, 'Do you want digital fabrication tools?', they won't know. If you ask, 'Do you want custom-furniture that matches your house?' or 'Do you want community-Internet that the users can extend?', then they'll say, 'Let me at it.' I think industry and academia do a terrible job of conveying the excitement of what you can do with this. Once people get access, they run with it.

What about Fab Labs in the UK?

In the UK the Manufacturing Institute charity completely gets the idea that the means of production are no longer scarce and the prototype has become the product. We've set up a Fab Lab with them in Manchester and are working to create more UK labs. What's working well in the UK is scaffolding, where communities can opt in, and it can expand and grow. It's an intermediate level, where there's enough operational support, but it is driven by bottom-up ownership, not top-down planning.

Which is democratic in a sense. Is it sufficient to get it going as a nourishing grass-roots environment?

There are a lot of frustrated UK innovators limited by existing industry. Manchester used to have three-quarters of the world's mills; it now has two football teams. One of the goals is to help start a new industrial revolution. One of the disappointments has been working with current businesses. They just want to use it to do whatever it is they've been doing, rather than to create new business.

> **You mentioned ownership. Are you following – or involved with – Open Design and the publicly shared licences of Creative Commons?**

In one sense it's exactly the same thing. This is open-source hardware. Protecting intellectual property [IP] only works when you can identify who is infringing. So it only works in an ecosystem with a barrier to access and limited participants. In the Fab Lab network anybody with access to a lab can infringe anything that anybody does in another lab. So we don't mandate IP, and people use various IP models. The point is that you are forced to work in an open way, because infringement is so easy that there's no way to ensure ownership. Sharing isn't imposed as a requirement, it's an operational consequence.

> **How do you view the proliferation of people and institutes that are opening different things with the word 'lab' attached to it?**

Well, we don't trademark Fab Lab, because we don't want to have to say Fab Lab™ everywhere. But we do curate the notion of labs as a distinguishable network to maintain standards. We don't own or try to control this area. But specifically with the Fab Lab network we want to make sure that there's a level of both technical and social engineering that they all meet ... so that anyone in any Fab Lab can do the same as at any other one.

> **So Maker Faires and the likes of the Open Design Lab in Berlin – these aren't part of the network?**

The people who run Maker Faire are good friends of ours. In fact, the first issue of *Make* magazine featured an interview with me in a Fab Lab. But Fab Lab capabilities go beyond what's typically assumed in the maker community. What defines the Fab Lab network is the evolution of technical capabilities to make complete functional systems that are shared, so that projects can be distributed across them. And then the social engineering – it's really the network of people and capabilities.

> **Are you a maker yourself? Do you use machines, and weld and solder? Is that part of your pleasure?**

Absolutely. Nobody gets away with being a manager in the Fab Lab network. It's hands-on for everyone. It's a very therapeutic process for everyone involved.

> **Now that the ideas about 3D fabrication and machines are replicating outside your lab, what type of making are you, at MIT, interested in?**

There's much too much attention given to 3D printing. In my lab at MIT I have every known

3D printer, and they are all expensive and slow. We make much more use of soft tooling. So we do subtractive machining, then make moulds and then cast materials like high-performance concrete, which lets you cheaply make large, strong three-dimensional parts. As a research road map, we're looking at 3D printing that can work in the field, but the labs focus on the shortest path to make things that perform well. There is a sense in which we cheat in a lot of ways. The Fab Lab doesn't do the molecular assembly, it sort of approximates what it's going to make.

Do you see this as counter to craft, though?

No. In fact, there's a story on that which is very relevant. Haystack School in the US is a temple of arts and crafts. It's one of the greatest architectural buildings in the country. It's in the woods in Maine, and it's where glass-blowers blow glass and paper-makers make paper. It's the high church of traditional crafts.

We did a residency there last summer. We brought a temporary lab, and it was so successful they made it permanent. And what happened? Half the people thought it was long overdue, and half thought, 'This doesn't belong here. We don't do computers.' It was a life-changing experience for many, but the computer wasn't really involved in the design process. They were designing with traditional media and then using the lab to turn their designs into what they wanted to make. So somebody would take a photograph of the light on the Maine ocean and turn it into a mould so that they could make glass that rippled like the sea. Or they would use the computer to turn ink designs into woodcuts. The lab was like a medium-converter. It was full of computing, but the computing wasn't used to design. It was used to map things from one media to another.

What's amazing is when untrained people have sudden access to these tools.

We're finding spectacular people who – given access to these capabilities – can do more, faster and better, than students at MIT. But by formal qualification they have no training, and they never found their way into the system. So we're finding the most amazing people with the most amazing skills who didn't have access to tools and didn't have a vehicle to discover them. One of the questions this poses is: is it for everyone, or is it elite? I guess you could call it democratically elite.

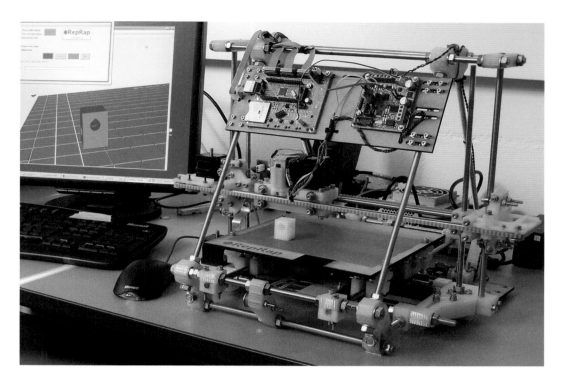

'RepRap' open-source
self-replicating
3D printer
Dr Adrian Bowyer
UK (Bath University)
2010

Photo courtesy
of RepRap

Polylactic acid plastic,
custom electronics

*Attempt to finish a thought
before it materializes
in front of your eyes.*

'Voidness' woven
audio-tape dress
Alyce Santoro (designer)
and Jeanette Santoro
(fabrication)
USA (Texas)
2008

Courtesy Museum
of Art, Rhode Island
School of Design
Photo by Erik Gould

Recorded audio cassette
tape, polyester thread,
velvet

*If nostalgia won't let you listen
To your old mixtapes
Make a dress out of that feeling.*

'Bloom'
Michael Eden
UK (Cumbria)
2010

Additive layer
manufacturing,
Rapid prototyping

Plaster and gypsum,
non-fired ceramic

After centuries of impersonation
the urn smashes
its domestic role
as historical succedaneum.

Children's custom toy
3D printer
Dejan Mitrovic
UK (London)
2010

Plastic, metal

Begin to play
by making friends
of many
different shapes.

Self-portrait machine
Jen Hui Liao
UK (London)

Photo by Jen Hui Liao

Plastic, metal

*Self-portrait of the artist
as a young medium
in a séance of the future.*

Wooden textile
Elisa Stroyzk
Germany (Berlin)
2010

Photo by Sebastian Neeb

Laser-cutting

Maple wood,
elaston cotton mix

*A malleable mountain range
to wrap around your shoulders
if you are cold
or feel immaterial.*

The Future of Making
Bruce Sterling

Home crafts and popular mechanics have deep roots. Dad's urge to tinker and Mum's keenness to knit are in no more danger than Mum and Dad themselves. We rarely see that our roots are also 'our future' – we perceive 'the future' as surprising new differences in life. We overlook our commonalities and continuities.

Some contemporary 'making' is very surprising indeed, while most is time-honoured stuff – homey, authentic, small-scale, handmade and pre-industrial. However, craftwork stands out more sharply now, against the gaudy background of modern high-tech production – what might be called the 'Total Work of Commerce'.

An object from the modern Total Work of Commerce is an integrated part of a product ecosystem. It enters our lives through brand management, the purchase experience, the ritual un-boxing. The goal of the Total Work of Commerce is to inveigle the user into a long-term relationship with the brand. Every 'touchpoint' is thought through with the care of a Disney thrill ride.

This sleek, stylish and comprehensive consumption-machine has never lacked rebels and doubters. It strikes certain people as cloying, invasive of privacy or ominously totalitarian. It does not bring an end of history, but is a period artefact, just like the production systems of the past. It cannot last, for it is physically unsustainable. Its resources are finite while its junkyard grows ever larger.

Closer study of any sleek consumer object will reveal a rickety, sprawling, multinational system of production whose driving forces can be repurposed. This is where the novelty lies; this is the 'futuristic' part of Making. This is why twenty-first-century Making veers sharply away from its ancestor, William Morris Arts and Crafts revivalism. The future of Making is in hacking the post-industrial milieu.

Every aspect of consumerism has a hacker shadow: a potential inversion, a repurposing. Consumerism, for instance, is keen on demographic buyer niche-targeting. 'Makerism' (to coin a term) is keen on niches of non-commercial enthusiasts. One or two hobby eccentrics in every town can find aid and succour in vast online communities. So folk-hobbies that might silently dwindle away – flint-knapping, cornhusk-weaving, scrimshaw – transform into social-network practices.

Old-fashioned television advertising mutates into 'vernacular video'. Almost anybody can shoot a brief Internet spot about some 'product' they have created and enjoy the pleasures of being admired, praised and maybe emulated. This is the traditional fuel of hobby crafts

– not that one builds ships in a bottle, but that people go 'Wow!' when they see it.

Global manufacturing is famous for lean, multinational, 'just-in-time' factory processes. Makers can now enjoy similar advantages; they too can browse the planet for just the right kind of crochet hook, enamel paint or chic transistor.

Commerce has its stern patents and copyrights, while Making enjoys louche, tolerant open-source and 'copyleft'. Patents and copyrights are alien to the Internet distribution system, commonly forcing for-profit corporations into abject, legally contorted positions of suing their own suppliers and harassing their own customers. By contrast, Instructables and free software can unite loose gangs of amateurs into formidable production networks.

Consumerism has Amazon, that mighty river of corporate goods, but 'Makerism' has Etsy, the global micromarket for personal crafts.

Every Maker scene has some set of tribal shamans widely acknowledged as maestros. If Motorola vanished tomorrow, few would shed a tear. However, if Linus Torvalds, creator of the Linux operating system, were to perish, there would be much rending of garments and tearing of hair. The Maker maestro sacrifices money for meaning, for mattering. The life of a maven does have its pleasures and seductions – especially when that social influence is digitized and globalized.

Corporations have contractual arrangements and business alliances. Makers have the API, or Application Programming Interface. This newfangled social custom (there really isn't a better term for it, though it is hugely important) allows cheap, flimsy, hobbyist software to interface directly with gigantic, professional, expensive software – such as, say, Google's software.

The API enables the signature accomplishment of modern Making, which is the 'mashup'. The 'mashup' uses an API to link large, sophisticated technological systems in small, inventive ways.

For instance, a Kinect videogame input device might be directly connected to a numerically controlled drill. Why would anyone 'mash' a videogame controller onto an industrial construction tool? Because it's cheap and easy to do – that's why. Because that feat attracts admiration. Because this ungainly hybrid might become a 'platform' for creating something else, which could itself be 'mashed'. Because a mashup is folk-art networking that is native to a Network Society.

The API enables giant enterprises – 'black boxes', vast congelations of human genius with millions of lines of code – to be

THE FUTURE OF MAKING IS IN HACKING THE POST-INDUSTRIAL MILIEU

used as trivial, low-cost components of homemade garage devices and services. We've reached an era whose technical devices are so blindingly complex that no single person, or even single discipline, can fully understand them. The API is the diplomatic solution to that complexity. The API allows our vast, buzzing systems to be hooked together like so many nineteenth-century railway cars. The modern Maker sees nothing hazardous or outré about the 'mashup'. The future Maker will be even more enthusiastic.

Making is a folk aspect of a great, unfolding struggle over humanity's means of information, production and distribution. This is a bigger struggle than the atelier of arts and crafts. The IED – Improvised Explosive Device – is Making as a military phenomenon. These crude but effective bombs are commonly a 'mashup' of cellphone components and purloined artillery shells.

The 'think-and-do lab' is Making as pedagogy. Cellphone revolutions are Maker politics. The list of parallels can be extended indefinitely. Behind these transformations are the cultural logics of a Network Society – the now-familiar change-drivers of massive computational power, wireless broadband, social software and search engines. No nation, people, institution, party or discipline is exempted from this transition. Even its enemies use its tools.

The folk-art of our Network Society will last as long as our 'network society' itself lasts – until our passing age is gathered unto the bosom of its ancestors, the Space Age and Atomic Age. The roots of folk-art will persist – ever ready to sprout, spread and grow, and no more frail than the grass that covers all.

i-LIHB pulse electronic
prosthetic arm
TouchBionics
UK (Livingstone)
2010

Aluminium,
high-density plastic

*At first contact, there was silence,
until we recognized their signals
and learned to speak in subtle impulses.*

Knitted dress
Sandra Backlund
Sweden (Stockholm)
2008

Photo by John Scarisback

Knitting

Wool

*Before you go to sleep
don't forget to switch your attire
from transmitter
to receiver mode.*

Woolfiller repairing fibre
Heleen Klopper
Netherlands (Amsterdam)
2009

Photo by Mandy Pieper

Foam, felt, needle,
coloured wool

Sugru hacking material
Jane ni Dhulchaointigh
UK (London)
2011

Silicone

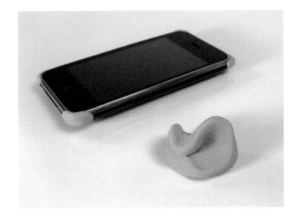

Make a feature out of a defect.
Fill every hole
with something better
than what was there before.

Forgive misfortune
or imperfection
with a clearly visible repair.

'E-shoe' wireless
high-heel guitar
Chicks on Speed
and Max Kibardin
2010

Photo by Gilmar Ribeiro

Industrial design,
electronics and
programming

Plastic, circuit board

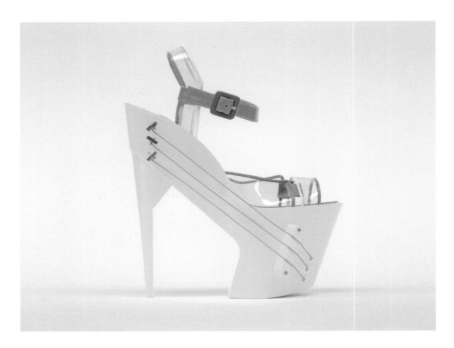

Strap your heels on,
check they're in tune,
flex your leg,
kick out the jams.

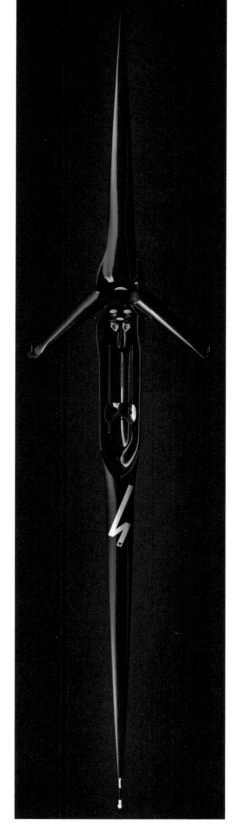

Stämpfli ST170
UK (Surrey)
2007

NOMEX aramid polymer,
carbon and glass fibre

'Detail.MGX' fingerprint
lampshade
Dan Yeffet
France (Paris)
Manufactured by .MGX,
Materialise N.V.
2007

Selective laser sintering,
rapid prototyping,
stereolithography

Polyamide (nylon),
stainless steel

*Perhaps the maker
inadvertently left
his fingerprint on the bulb
and it bloomed overnight.*

*Hardly any weight,
just trajectory,
around the body of the rower.*

Glossary of Techniques and Processes

The terms included in this glossary have been selected from the skills and techniques used to make objects displayed in the *Power of Making* exhibition. This modest list only touches upon the total number, range and diversity of skills and techniques being used across the globe today.

3D animation: using computer software to create and animate a three-dimensional representation of image data.

3D printing: printing individual layers of plaster or resin to form a three-dimensional object.

3D scanning: digitally recording the three-dimensional properties of an object to create a *computer-aided design* file.

3D visualization: using computer software to produce images, diagrams or animations that represent the form of a three-dimensional object. May involve *3D scanning* or *3D animation*.

Additive manufacturing: building up material layer by layer to form three-dimensional objects. Includes *rapid prototyping*.

Airbrushing: spraying a material with paint using a handheld compressed-air spray gun. Known as *spray-painting* when using a larger spray gun.

Annealing: heating glass or metal before cooling it slowly, to relieve internal stresses or alter the material's physical properties.

Baking: cooking by dry heat, typically in an oven, to transform the physical properties of a material.

Beading: decorating or covering with beads. Also: veneer beading involves attaching a thin layer of wooden edging around an object to create an attractive finish. See also *veneering*.

Blacksmithing: heating iron or steel before shaping it through *forging*, *welding* or *heat-treating*. Includes *drawing* and *hammering*.

Bleaching: using chemicals (usually a solution of sodium hypochlorite or hydrogen peroxide) to whiten materials.

Blocking: pressing and steaming an unfinished hat against a wooden mould or flange to style and shape it.

Boring: making a hole in or through a material or object.

Brazing: joining two or more close-fitting parts with a molten filler metal. Similar to *soldering*, but takes place at higher temperatures (above 450°C).

Carpentry: making or repairing things in wood.

Carving: cutting and removing material (usually wood or stone) to form an object, pattern or inscription.

Casting: shaping molten material (usually plaster, metal or glass) by pouring it into a mould.

Checkering: carving lines to create textured 'non-slip' patterns (usually on the finished wooden handgrips of guns).

Clicking: using a shaped blade, punch or die to cut metal or leather cleanly. A form of *die-cutting*.

Cobbling: repairing shoes. The making of shoes is known as *cordswaining*.

Coding: see *programming*.

Computer-aided design (CAD): using computer software to design an object.

Computer-aided manufacture (CAM): using computer software to control a machine, tool or process.

Computer numerical control (CNC): using computer software to automate machine tools.

Construction: building an object or structure.

Coopering: making or repairing barrels and casks.

Cordswaining: making shoes. The repairing of shoes is known as *cobbling*.

Counted-thread embroidering: hand-stitching on fabric, over a pre-determined number of threads. Includes *needlepoint* and *petit point*.

Crocheting: interlocking a loop of yarn or wool with another to make fabric using a hooked needle. Differs from *knitting* because only one loop is active at any time.

Cross-stitch: *sewing* or *embroidering* using two stitches that cross over one other.

Cutting: removing material with a knife.

Cutting in: using a heading knife to cut the slope of a barrel or cask top section.

Die-cutting: using a shaped blade, punch or die to cut metal, rubber, textiles or paper cleanly. Known as *clicking* when applied to metal or leather.

Digitizing: converting data into a digital form, to be processed by computer software.

Draughtsmanship: see *technical drawing*.

Drawing: lengthening a piece of soft metal, usually by *hammering*. Also: making marks and lines on paper, usually with a pen and pencil. *Technical drawing* involves detailed plans and specifications.

Dressing out: smoothing the inside wall of a barrel or cask.

Drilling: making a hole in or through a material or object by *boring* with a drill.

Dry-stone walling: selecting and placing stones to build or repair stone walls without mortar or cement.

Dyeing: adding colour by soaking material in a solution containing dye.

Embroidering: *sewing* patterns on to fabric with thread to create a decorative pattern.

Etching: engraving (usually metal, glass or stone) by scratching through a protective layer, before using acid to burn away exposed sections.

Felting: rolling and pressing fibrous material (usually wool) with heat and moisture, to form a smooth surface. Known as *planking* when applied to *hatting*.

Filigree: twisting threads of wire (usually silver or gold) into delicate ornamental patterns.

Filing: using a file to smooth or shape a surface.

Finishing: producing an attractive or functional surface to complete the manufacture or decoration of an object.

Firing: using a high-temperature kiln to fuse together particles within, or on, pottery to form hard and strong ceramics.

Flameworking: see *lampworking*.

Forging: heating metal in a fire or furnace before *hammering* it to form an object.

Free embroidering: hand-stitching on fabric without regard to the weave. Differs from *counted-thread embroidering*, which stitches over a specific number of threads.

Fusing: joining or blending materials to form a single entity.

Fusion bonding: rolling strands of natural hair together with human-hair extensions and a warm keratin material to form a strong protein bond.

Glass-blowing: blowing semi-molten glass through a long tube to make glassware.

Glassing: combining woven or felted glass fabric with a plastic resin to form a hard, protective fibre-glass coating. Also known as fibre-glassing.

Glazing: coating pottery or metal with powdered glass, which is heated in a kiln to create a smooth, decorative and waterproof surface.

Grinding: applying abrasive friction to sharpen, smooth or form an object.

Hammering: hitting or beating metal with a hammer.

Hatting: making hats. May involve *planking, pouncing* and *blocking*. *Millinery* refers to the making of women's hats.

Heat-treating: using heating or chilling to harden or soften metal or glass. Includes *annealing*.

Hot glass working: manipulating glass in a direct flame. Includes *glass-blowing* and *lampworking*.

Incising: making a cut or series of cuts into a material to mark or decorate it.

Investment casting: casting molten metal in a ceramic mould formed around a wax model. The wax is melted away before casting; the ceramic mould is destroyed to access the cast object.

Joinery: cutting and fitting wood joints without using nails.

Knitting: interlocking loops of yarn or wool to make fabric using two knitting needles or a machine.

Knotting: tying knots in thread or yarn to make fabric.

Lace-making: looping, twisting or braiding thread (usually cotton) to form fabric with open holes.

Lacquering: covering material with a liquid that dries to form a hard protective surface.

Laminating: joining one or more layers of material together. Can be used for the same material or to combine different materials.

Lampworking: using a gas torch to melt glass (most commonly soda-lime and borosilicate) and moulding, cutting or blowing it into different shapes. Also known as torch-working or flameworking.

Laser-cutting: cutting through material (usually plastic, textile, wood or cardboard) or engraving a pattern on a surface using a laser controlled by a *computer-aided design* file.

Lathing: see *wood-turning*.

Locksmithing: making or repairing locks.

Lock-stitching: interlocking an upper thread with a lower bobbin thread on a sewing machine. Also known as single needle stitching.

Marquetry: inlaying small pieces of coloured wood (traditionally to decorate furniture).

Metal spinning: see *spinning*.

Millinery: making women's hats.

Milling: cutting or shaping metal with a power-driven rotating tool. Can include *drilling* and *threading*.

Modelling: shaping a malleable material to form a three-dimensional object.

Moulding: shaping an easily manipulated material using a rigid frame or model to form an object with a particular shape.

Mould-making: forming a pliable material into a hollow, rigid shape that will be filled with a *casting* liquid.

Needlepoint: stitching yarn through an open-weave canvas, generally using tent stitch. A form of *counted-thread embroidery*. Also includes *petit point*.

Ornamental turning: using cutting tools to create complex forms and shapes on a fixed work, by repositioning the tool or object. Differs from *wood-turning* because the object may not be spinning.

Painting: covering a material with paint to create a decorative or protective surface.

Panel-beating: hand-*hammering* of metal to form or finish smooth, hollow shapes.

Paper-making: draining a suspension of fibres (usually wood pulp) through a screen to form a mat of interwoven fibres, which is then *pressed* and dried.

Pattern-cutting: creating clothing pattern templates from working drawings.

Pattern-welding: welding different metals together in a forge and twisting them to form a patterned 'Damascus steel' blade.

Petit point: stitching yarn through a very fine open-weave canvas. A form of *needlepoint* and *counted-thread embroidery*.

Planking: hardening the raw material of a hat by *felting*.

Polishing: rubbing, to form a smooth and shiny surface.

Pouncing: *sanding* felt hats to create a smooth finish.

Pressing: applying pressure to flatten, shape or smooth a material.

Programming: designing, writing and testing computer software programs. Also known as coding.

Punching: making holes or impressing a design in a material (usually paper, leather and metal).

Quilting: joining together layers of fabric and padding with lines of stitching.

Rapid prototyping: using computer software and specialist hardware to automate the construction of three-dimensional objects. Includes *3D printing*, *selective laser sintering* and *stereolithography*.

Retouching: making slight additions or alterations to improve or repair an object.

Rotational moulding: heating powdered or liquid plastic in a mould, which is then rotated around two axes to create hollow objects. Also known as roto-moulding or rotocasting.

Saddlery: making or repairing saddles, bridles and other equestrian equipment.

Sanding: using abrasive sandpaper or a mechanical sander to smooth and *polish* a surface.

Sawing: using a long, thin serrated blade in a back-and-forward movement to cut wood (or other hard material).

Scoring: cutting or scratching a notch or line on an object.

Sculpting: shaping material by *carving* or *casting*.

Selective laser sintering (SLS): computer-controlling a moving laser beam to coalesce a powdered material (usually plastic or metal) into a solid mass, forming a three-dimensional object, layer by layer.

Sewing: joining, fastening or repairing by making stitches with thread. Also known as stitching.

Sheet-rolling: passing metal through a pair of rollers to form thin sheets.

Silver-plating: coating an object with silver, usually by electroplating.

Single needle stitching: see *lock-stitching*.

Slumping: heating glass in a kiln to make a flexible solid form. A form of warm *glass working*.

Smithing: see *blacksmithing*.

Soldering: joining two materials with a low-melting alloy (usually based on lead and tin). Similar to *brazing*, but takes place at lower temperatures (below 450°C).

Spin-forming: see *spinning*.

Spinning: applying force to a metal disc or tube rotating at high speed to form an axially symmetric object. Also known as spin-forming or metal-spinning.

Spray-painting: spraying a material with paint under pressure to create a decorative or protective surface. Known as *airbrushing* when using a handheld spray gun.

Stamping: pressing a die against a material to impress a pattern or mark. Used in leather and sheet-metal work.

Steam-bending: softening strips of wood by exposure to steam, to bend them around a mould.

Steaming: softening the stave boards of a barrel by exposure to steam. See also *steam-bending*.

Steel-folding: joining hundreds of layers of different grades of steel through *forging*.

Stereolithography: computer-controlling a moving laser beam to harden liquid polymer and form a three-dimensional object, layer by layer.

Stitching: see *sewing*.

Stone-setting: securing gemstones within jewellery.

Stop-motion animation: imaging a scene or object across a number of small incremental movements.

Striking up: *filing* and *sanding* the unfinished barrels of a shotgun to create a smooth, even surface ready for *polishing*.

Subtractive manufacturing: removing or shaping material to form three-dimensional objects. Includes *wood-turning, boring, drilling, sawing* and *tapping*.

Sugar-blowing: blowing or pumping air onto warm sugar to form shapes.

Sugar working: manipulating hot sugar. Includes *sugar-blowing*, pulling and spinning.

Superforming: using a vacuum to stretch a heated sheet of aluminium over a mould to create an object. Known as *vacuum-forming* when applied to other materials.

Tailoring: making fitted clothes.

Tapestry weaving: *weaving* on a vertical loom. Differs from cloth weaving because the warp threads are hidden in the finished piece. Weaving may also be completed in sections rather than working from one side to the other.

Tapping: drilling a hole and cutting a screw thread on its inside surface.

Technical drawing: creating detailed standardized plans or drawings, which specify the form of an object. Also known as draughtsmanship.

Threading: creating a screw thread. Includes *grinding, milling* and *tapping* approaches.

Throwing: pressing, squeezing and pulling clay rotating on a potter's wheel to form radially symmetric ceramics.

Tinning: covering or coating an object with tin. Also: a stage in *soldering*.

Torchworking: see *lampworking*.

Transfer-printing: printing on specially coated paper, which is then used to apply an image to a curved or uneven surface. Usually applied to textiles or pottery.

Trussing: using truss hoops to bend the *steamed* stave boards of a cask or barrel.

Vacuum-forming: using a vacuum to stretch a heated sheet of plastic or metal over a mould to create an object. When applied to aluminium it is known as *superforming*.

Varnishing: covering wood or other materials with varnish to create a hard, clear, shiny surface.

Veneering: attaching thin layers of fine wood onto coarse wood or board to create an attractive finish. See also *beading*.

Warm glass working: manipulating glass by heating it in a kiln. Includes *casting* and *slumping*.

Weaving: interlacing threads of yarn, wool or fabric passing in one direction (the weft) with threads secured at a right angle (the warp), to form fabric.

Welding: joining together metals by melting their surfaces, *pressing* and *hammering*.

Wicker working: plaiting or *weaving* twigs of willow to make baskets and furniture.

Wood-turning: using a stationary cutting tool to cut a wooden object that is spinning rapidly on a lathe.

Notes

1 See 'Introduction: Foundation of a Theory of the Body', in Donn Welton, *The Body* (Oxford, 1999), pp.1–6

2 Pamela H. Smith, *The Body of the Artisan: Art and experience in the scientific revolution* (Chicago, 2004), p.100

3 Ibid., p.98

4 See, for example, the comments by James Dyson, interviewed by Rebecca Smithers, 'Will design and technology survive the curriculum review?', *Education Guardian* (April 2011), p.4

5 Howard Gardner, *Frames of Mind: The theory of multiple intelligences* (London, 1985), pp.210, 4

6 Smith (2004), p.103

7 Ibid., p.103

8 For example, Richard Sennett, *The Craftsman* (London, 2008); Matthew Crawford, *The Case for Working with Your Hands* (London, 2009); Shu Hung and Joseph Magliaro (eds) *By Hand: The use of craft in contemporary art* (New York, 2007); Maria Elena Buszek (ed.), *Extra/Ordinary: Craft and contemporary art* (Durham, NC, 2011)

9 For example, Mihaly Csikszentmihalyi, *Flow: The psychology of optimal experience* (New York, 1991), and Mihaly Csikszentmihalyi, *Creativity* (London, 1996); Peter Dormer, *The Art of the Maker* (London, 1994)

10 Smith (2004), p.99

11 David Pye, *The Nature and Art of Workmanship* (Cambridge, 1968), see in particular pp.24, 75, 83–6

12 Virginia Postrel, *The Substance of Style: How the rise of aesthetic value is remaking culture, commerce and consciousness* (London, 2003), p.24

13 Ibid., p.24

14 Mark M. Smith, *Sensory History* (Oxford, 2007), p.3

15 Michel Serres, *The Five Senses*, cited in David Howes, *Empire of the Senses: The sensual culture reader* (Oxford, 2004)

16 Bernard Leach, *A Potter's Book* (London, 1940; reprinted paperback edition 1977), p.17

17 Michel Foucault *The Use of Pleasure: A History of Sexuality*, vol.2 (Harmondsworth, 1992), pp.8–9

18 Quoted in Lee Ufan, *The Art of Encounter* (London, 2008)

19 drpop.org/democracy/dit-do-it-together

20 Richard Sennett, *The Craftsman* (Harmondsworth, 2009)

21 furtherfield.org/furtherstudio/docs/about.html

22 Eric S. Raymond, *The Cathedral & the Bazaar: Musings on Linux and Open Source by an Accidental Revolutionary* (Sebastopol, CA, 1999)

23 castoff.info/album/02circle_line/pages/01.asp

24 dorkbot.org

25 mztek.org

26 instructables.com/id/tilt-sensing-quilt

27 from Fab Lab Manchester, fablabmanchester.org

28 from FabCentral website, fab.cba.mit.edu/

Further reading

19 Pulgadas, Patricia Rodriguez
(El Aleph Editores, Barcelona, 2008)

The Art of Not Making: The New Artist/Artisan Relationship, Michael Petry (Thames & Hudson, 2011)

The Art of the Maker: Skill and Its Meaning in Art, Craft and Design, Peter Dormer
(Thames & Hudson, 1994)

Beyond the Dovetail: Craft, Skill and Imagination
Christopher Frayling (Crafts Council, 1991)

'Can Britain Still Make It', Daniel Charny, in
Design in Britain: Big Ideas (Small Island),
ed. Deyan Sudjic (Conran Octopus, 2009)

The Craft Reader, Glenn Adamson (ed.)
(Berg Publishers, 2009)

The Crafts in Britain in the Twentieth Century
Tanya Harrod (Yale University Press, 1999)

The Craftsman, Richard Sennet (Penguin Press, 2009)

On Craftsmanship: Towards a New Bauhaus
Christopher Frayling (Oberon Masters, 2011)

Do It, Hans Ulrich Obrist (ed.)
(e-flux & Revolver, 2004)

Extra/Ordinary: Craft and Contemporary Art
Maria Elena Buszek (ed.) (Duke University Press, 2011)

*FAB: The Coming Revolution on Your Desktop –
From Personal Computers to Personal Fabrication*
Neil Gershenfeld (Basic Books, 2005)

*Hand + Made: The Performative Impulse in Art
and Craft*, Valerie Cassel Oliver (ed.)
(Contemporary Arts Museum, Houston, 2010)

Journal of Modern Craft, Glenn Adamson,
Edward S. Cooke, Jr, and Tanya Harrod (eds)
(Berg Publishers, 2008)

Makers, Cory Doctorow (Harper Voyager, 2009)

*Making It: Manufacturing Techniques
for Product Design*, Chris Lefteri
(Laurence King, 2007)

*The Making of Design: From the First Model to
the Final Product*, Gerrit Terstiege
(Birkhäuser Verlag AG, 2009)

Objects and Meaning, Anna Fariello and Paula Owen
(eds) (The Scarecrow Press, Inc., 2004)

Open Design Now, Bas van Abel, Lucas Evers,
Roel Klaassen, Peter Troxler (ed.) (BIS Publishers, 2011)

Shaping Things, Bruce Sterling (MIT Press, 2005)

*Shop Class as Soulcraft: An Inquiry into the Value
of Work*, Matthew B. Crawford (Penguin Press, 2009)

Stuff, Daniel Miller (Polity Press, 2009)

*String, Felt, Thread: The Hierarchy of Art and
Craft in American Art*, Elissa Auther
(University of Minnesota Press, 2009)

Thinking Through Craft, Glenn Adamson
(Berg Publishers, 2007)

Tord Boontje, Martina Margetts (Rizzoli, 2007)

The Variable Man, Philip K. Dick (Sphere Books, 1969)

http://www.open-source-embroidery.org.uk
Ele Carpenter

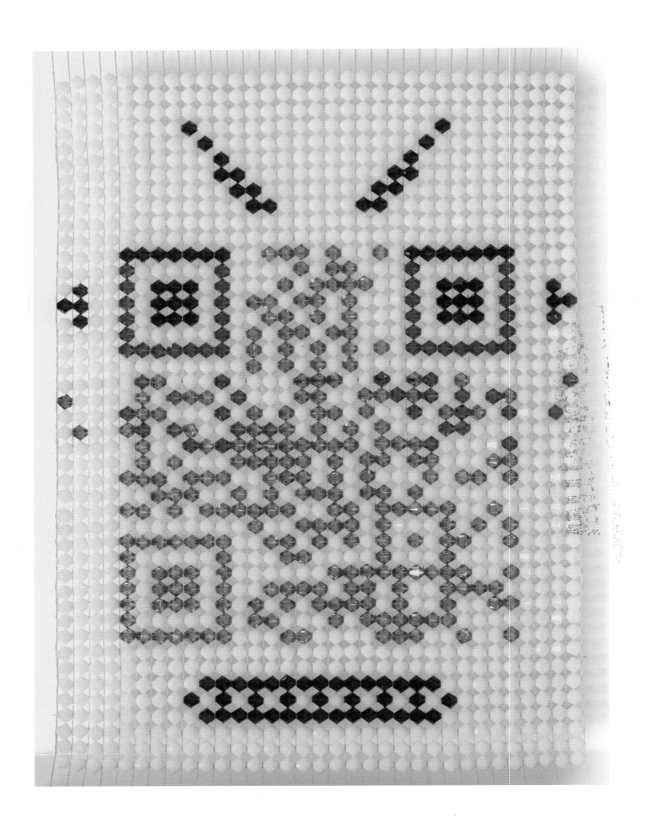

'QR U?' custom-made tag
for Power of Making
Thorunn Arnadottir
UK (London)
2011

Swarovski crystals and
thread

Beadwork and digitizing